Coloring book for adults and kids
beautiful building   design

This coloring book is belongs to

____

____

____

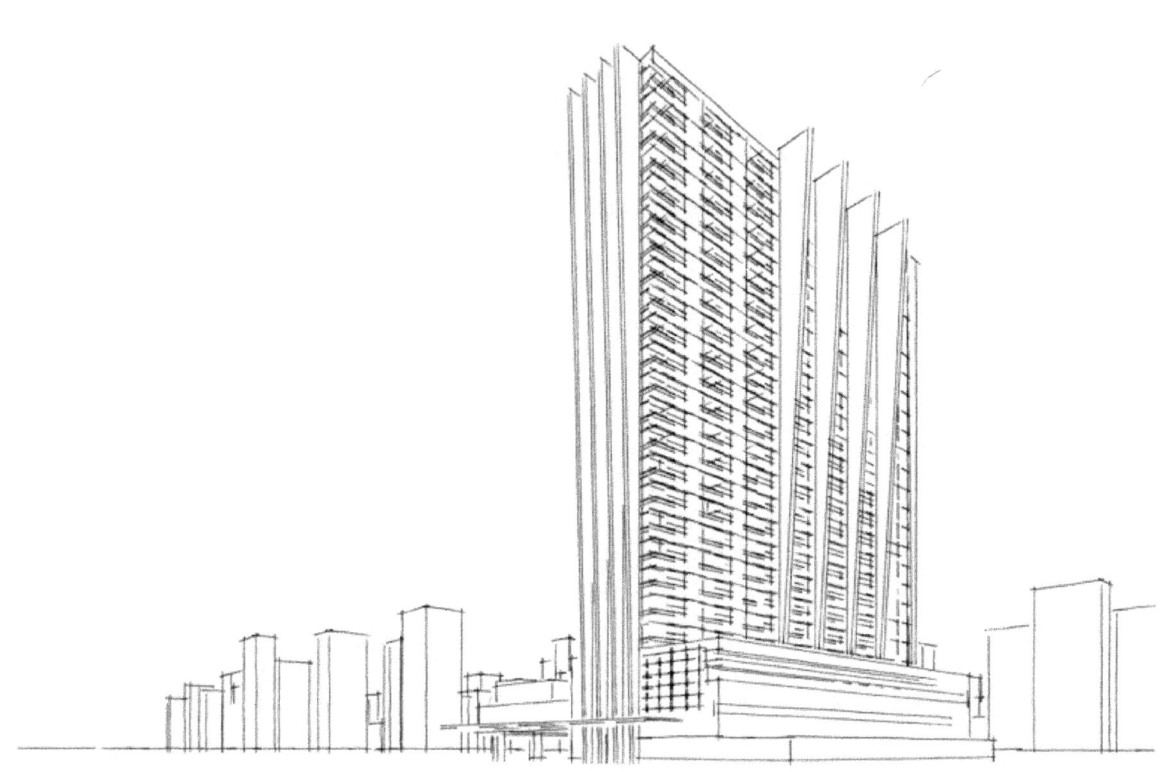

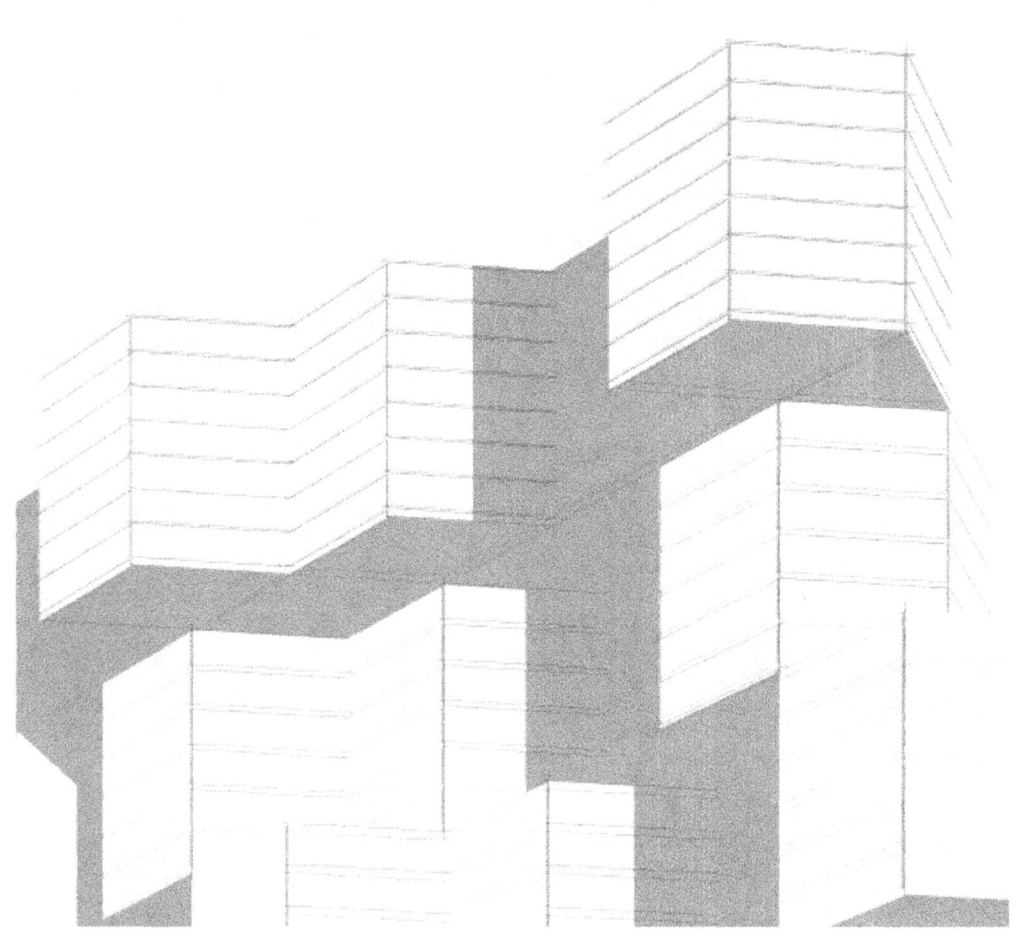

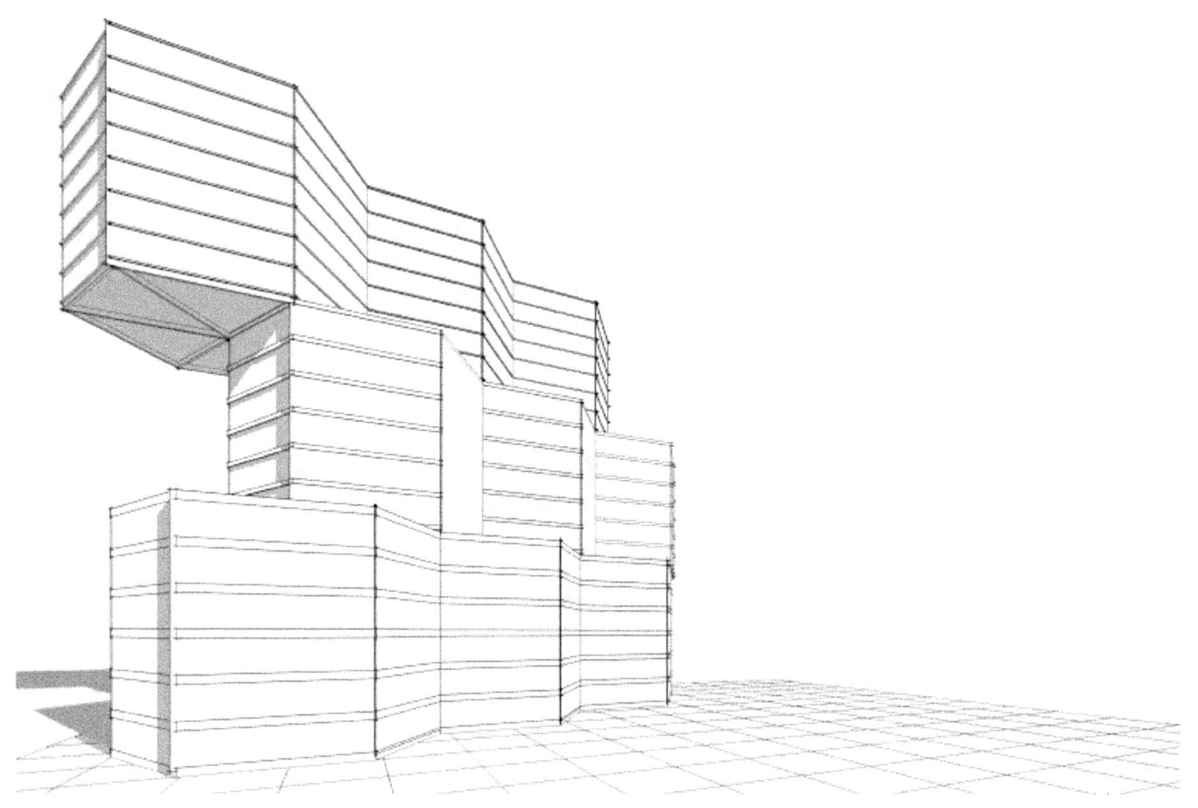

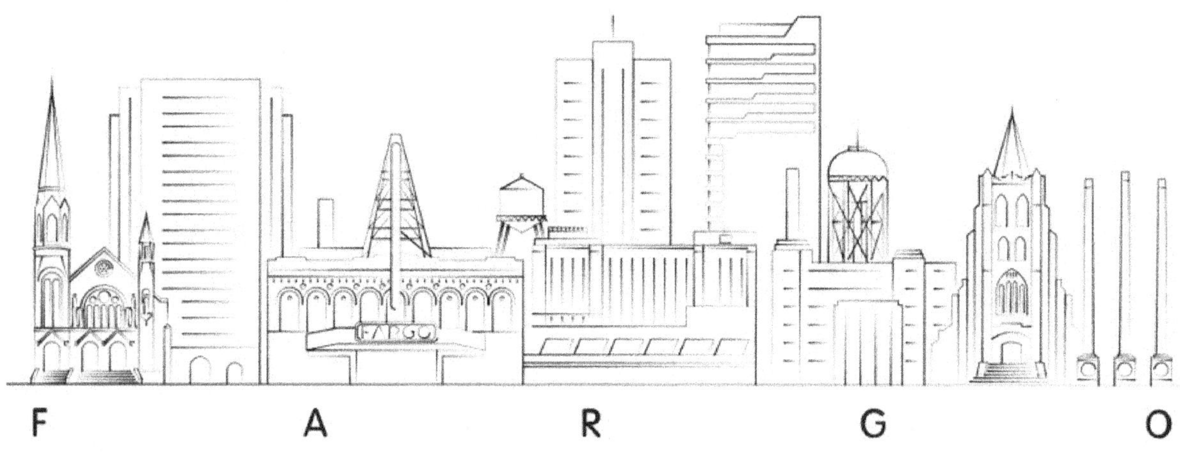
F   A   R   G   O

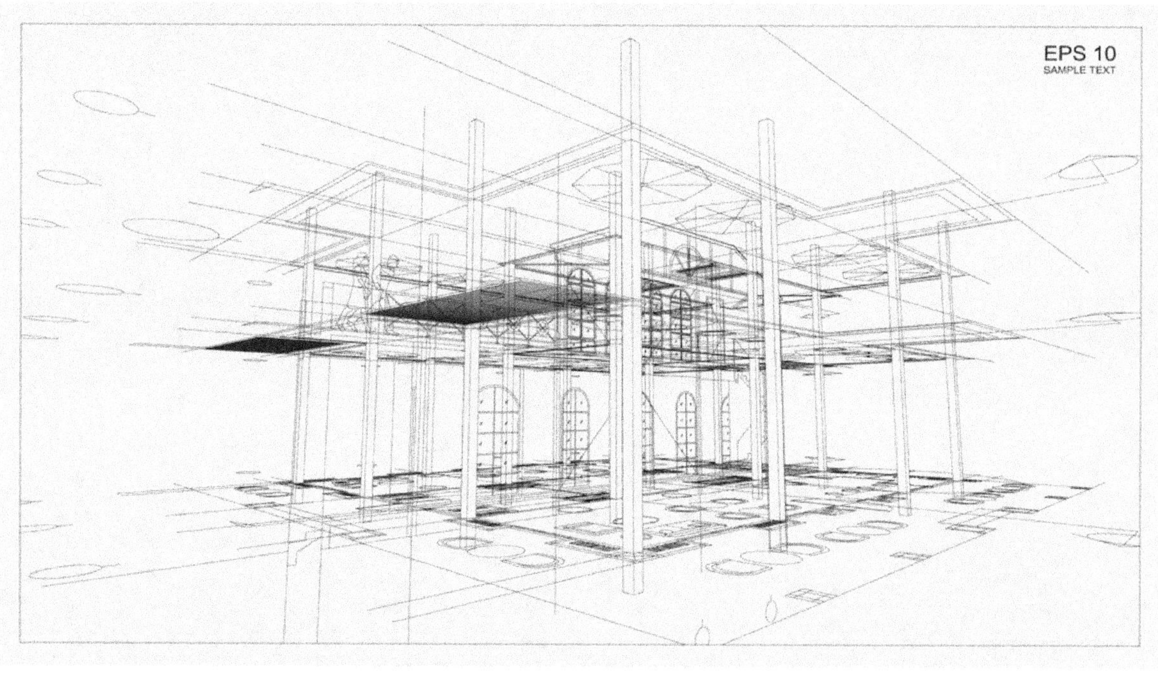
EPS 10
SAMPLE TEXT

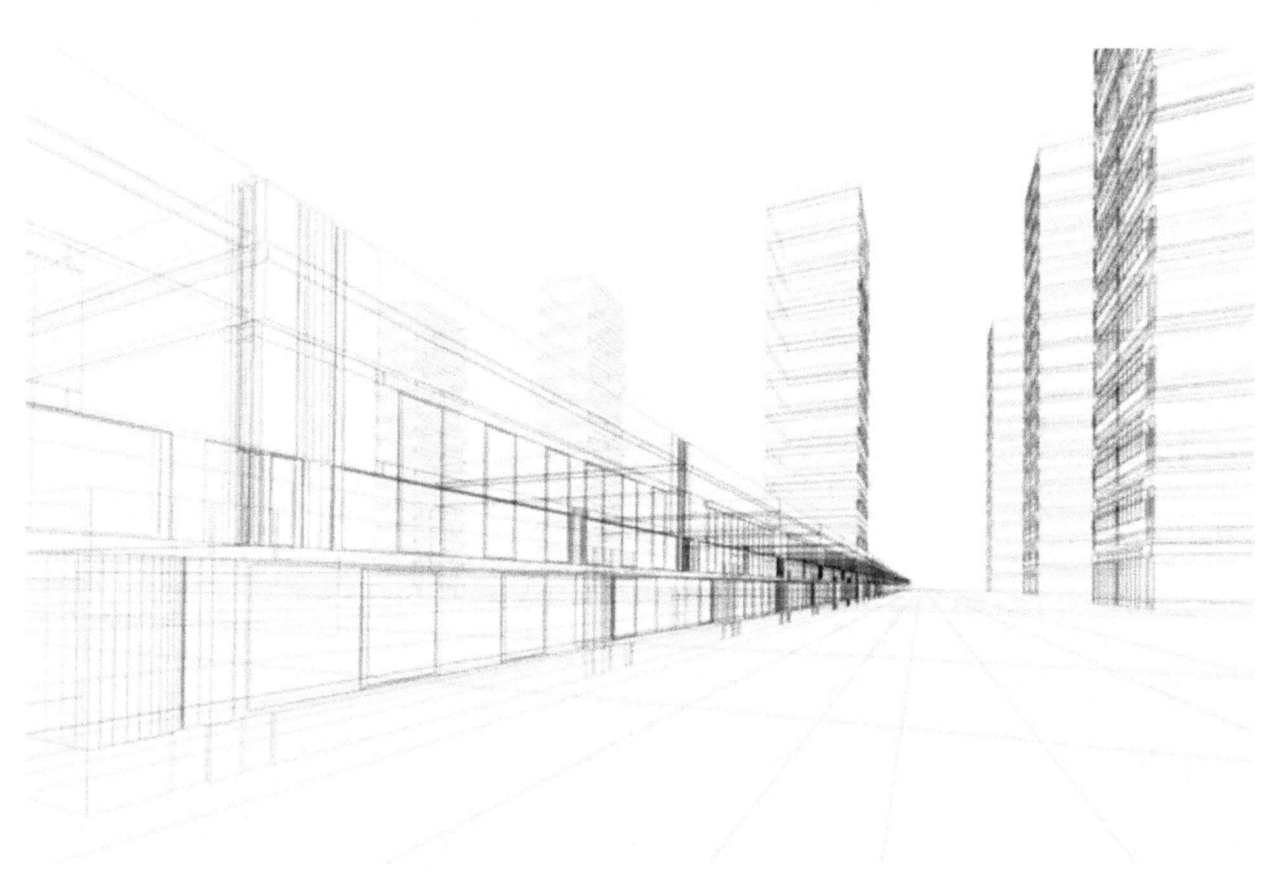

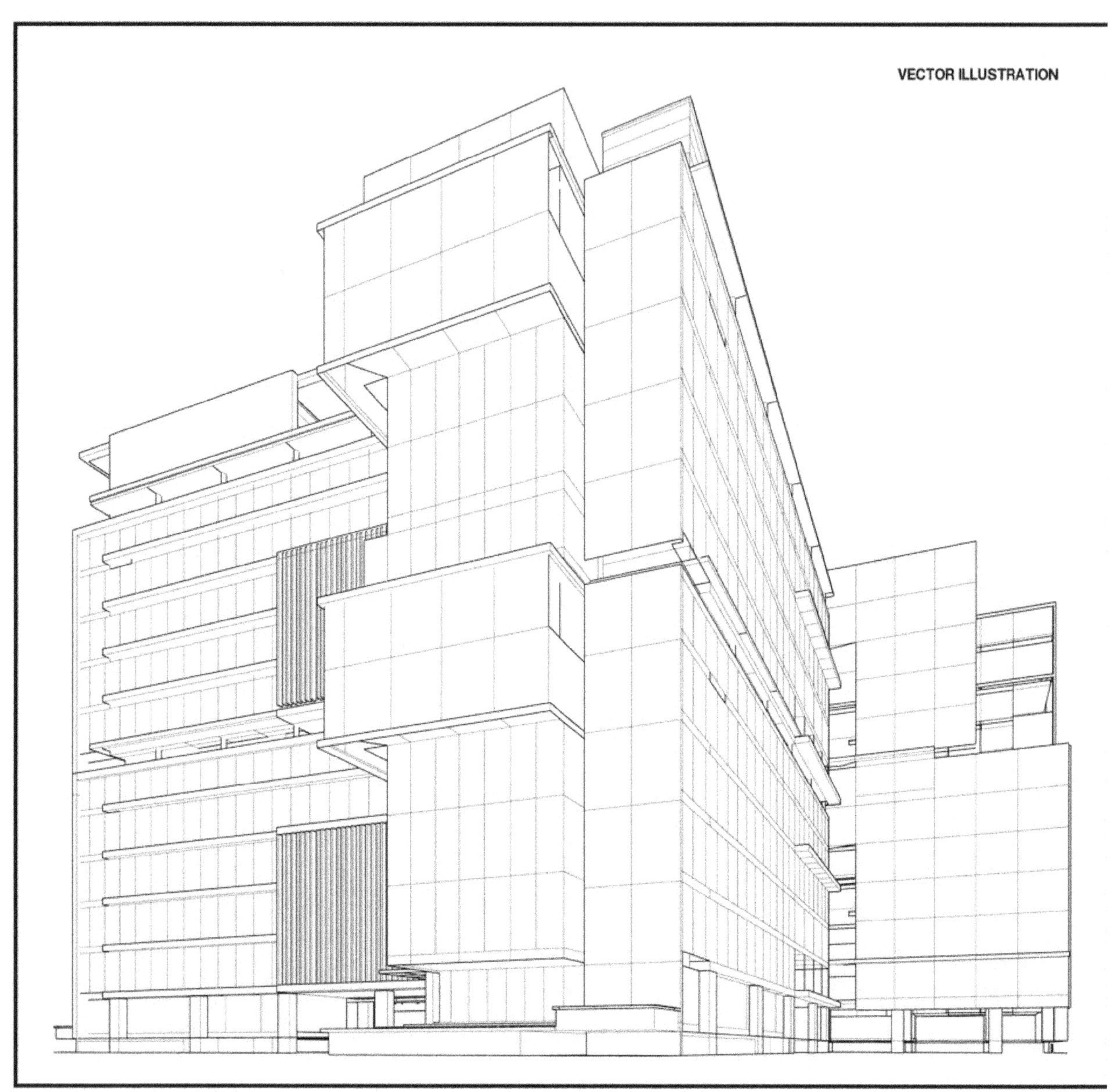
VECTOR ILLUSTRATION

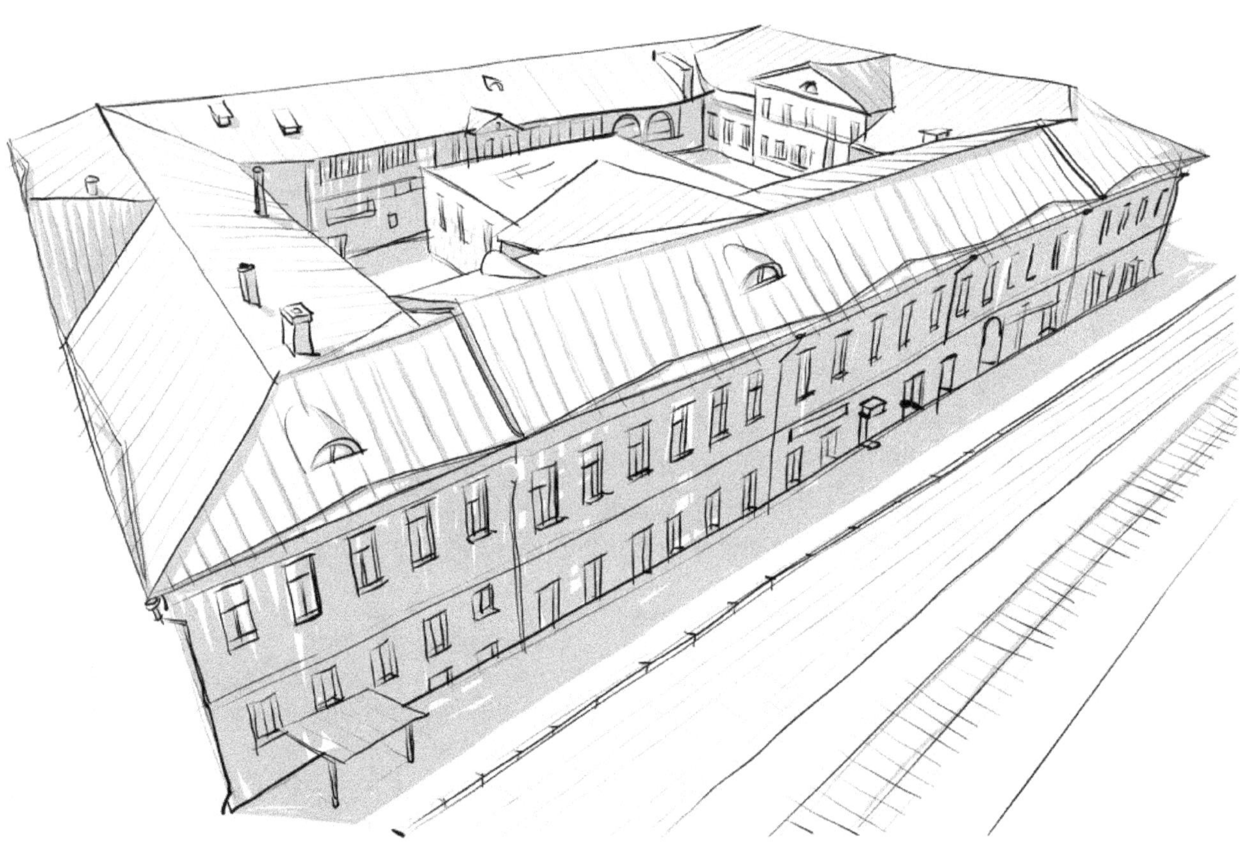

BUILDING VECTOR
architecture background

BUILDING WIREFRAME
vector eps 10

VECTOR ILLUSTRATION

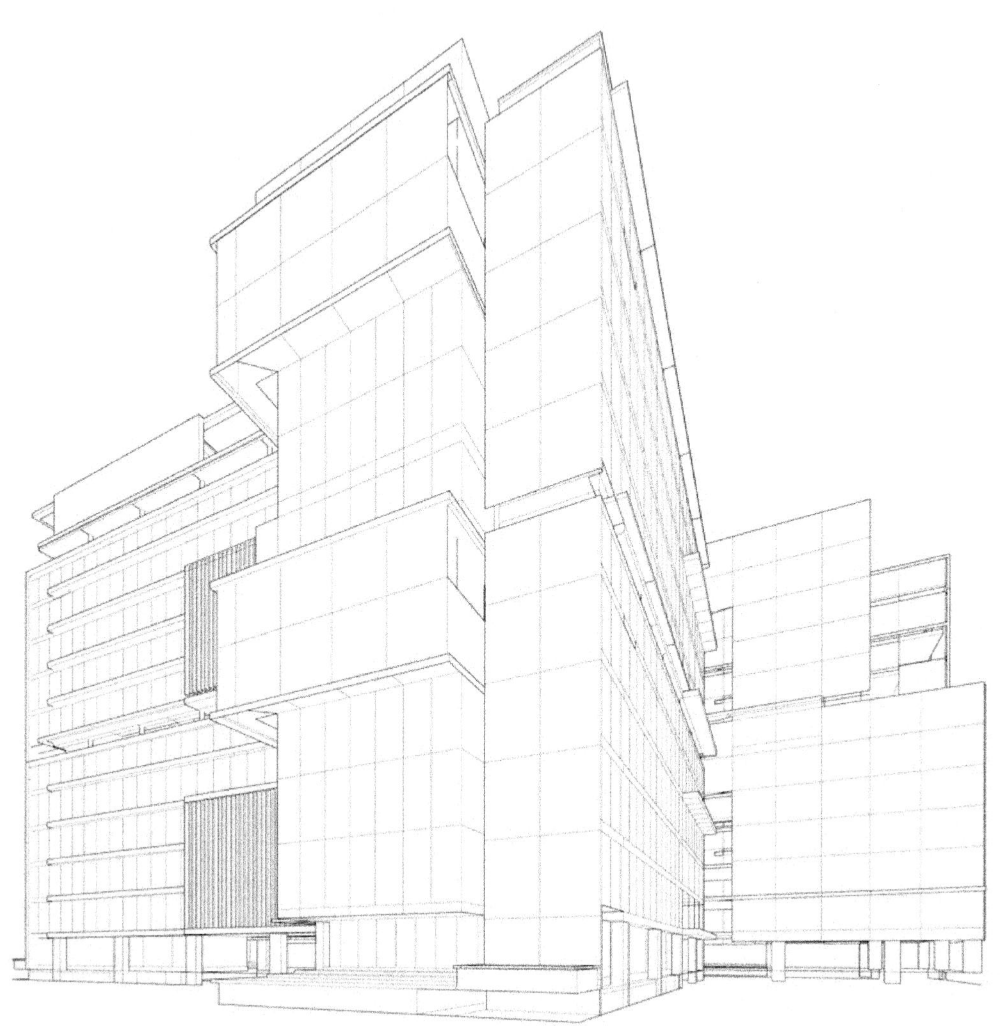

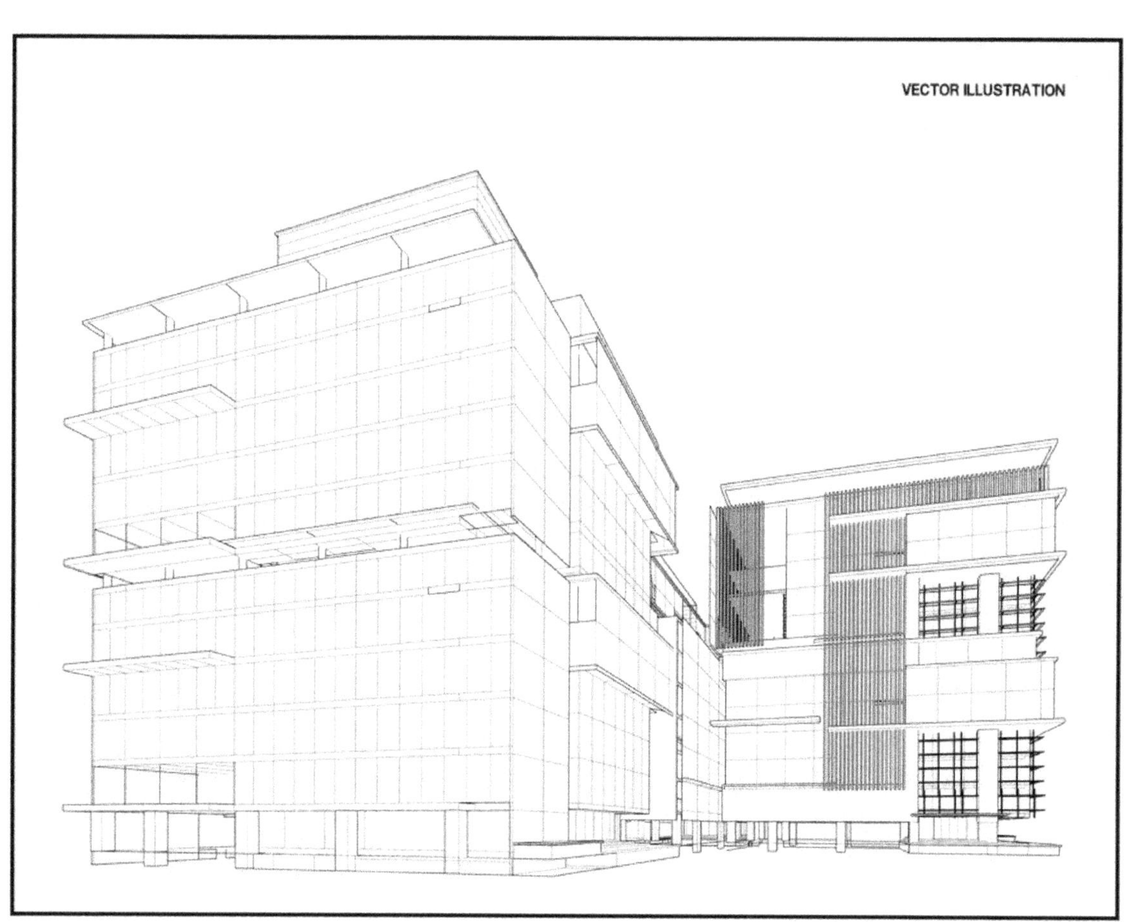
VECTOR ILLUSTRATION

LLUSTRATION

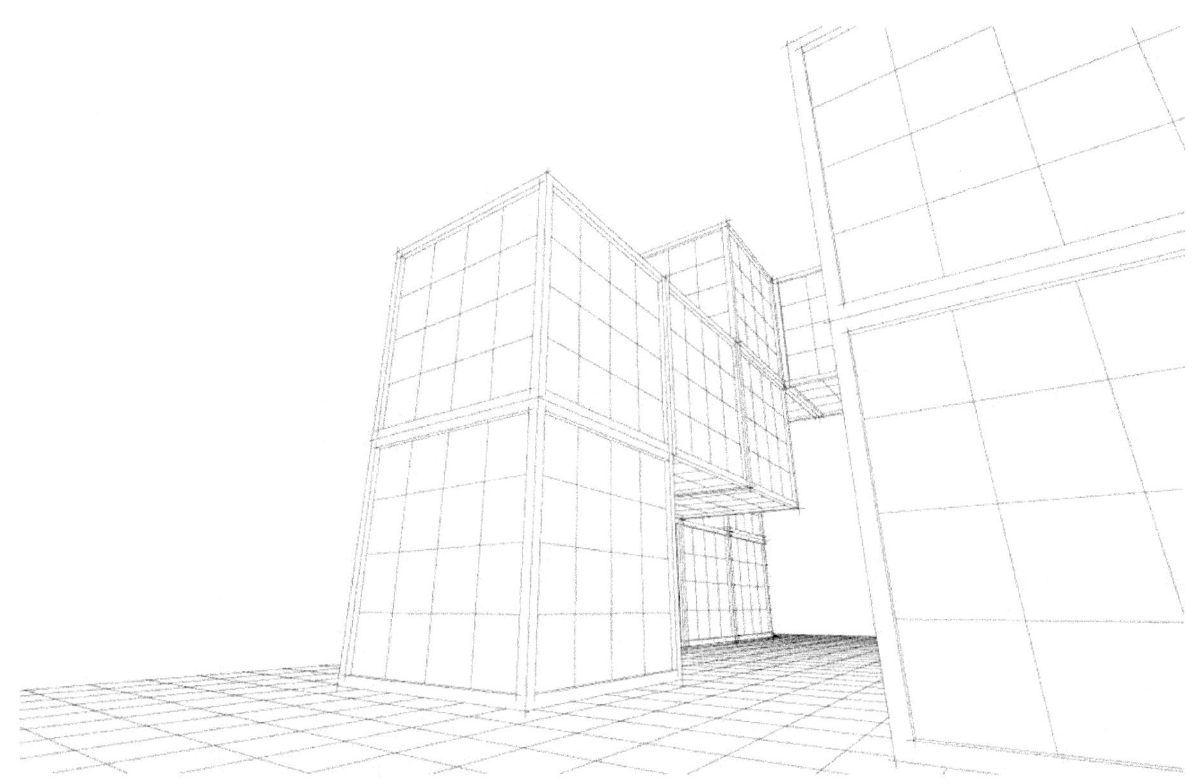

ARCHITECTURE BACKGROUND
VECTOR ILLUSTRATION